A QUESTION OF SURVIVAL

A QUESTION OF SURVIVAL

Richard Moore

University of Georgia Press, Athens

Acknowledgments

The author and the publisher gratefully acknowledge permission to reprint these poems which originally appeared in the publications here noted: "Thoughts of a Voyeur," *The American Scholar*; "Abroad" and "Hawks," *The Atlantic Monthly*; "Of Silence," "Stumps," and "The Swarm," *Denver Quarterly*; "Hymn to an Automatic Washer," "Psychiatric Discharges," "To a Poet," "To a Successful Student," and "To One on Friendly Terms with Many Poets," *Harper's Magazine*; "War Wife," *The Listener*; "Branches," "The Conquest," "Of a Young Mother," and "Spring Thaw," *Mademoiselle*; "Apparition," "Drought," "Makers," and "Suburb Hilltop," *The New Yorker* (copyright 1964 by The New Yorker Magazine, Inc.); "Canzone for a Tower," "Doctor Cat," "Memoir of a Pilot," "An Old Performer," "To a Poetess-Judge," and "A Way Out," *Perspective*; "Beyond the Atlantic," "Home News," "Summer House," and "Sunset," *Poetry Northwest*; "Sunlight at Work," "Terra Firma," "To a Child with a Top," "The Watch," and "Willy," *The Reporter*; "Dactyllic Discourse," "Epitaph for a Learned Poetess," "The Gem," "In Memory of an Overambitious Poem," and "Leaves at Night," *Saturday Review* (Copyright 1957, 1958, 1963, 1965 by the Saturday Review, Inc.); "Jungle War," *Supernation at Peace and War* by Dan Wakefield (Copyright 1968 by Little, Brown); "Elegy," *Transatlantic Review*; "Birth in Sussex," "Flies," "In Lieu of Sleep," and "Struggle," *The Virginia Quarterly Review.*

For my mother and in memory of my father

Contents

III   APPARITIONS

IV   SQUIBS

V   CREATURES

VI   MEMOIR OF A PILOT

I PROSPECTS

A Way Out

I watch the sun out of cloud sink
down to the west horizon's brink
from the hill here, an empty place,
and watch leaves crossing the sun's face
and think of melancholy lines—
but, there below, our gaudy city shines
and the insurance company's tower pops
up like a corsetted, five-hundred-eyed Cyclops,
solemn, imitating a steeple . . .

Was there ever a serious, a devout me?
O, when I think of all the people
with absurd opinions about me,
including myself—reader, I feel
called upon to confess
that I'm essentially pure nothingness
and that this lust I feel to be contained
at bottom may be frivolous and feigned.
I don't mean I'm an ethereal soul.
No, I'm more like an axle-hole
with small desires to become a Wheel:
the inmost me,
shapeless capacity,

shrinking from where the prisons are,
inside a hollowed rock or earthen jar
or, in this Age of Metal,
a pressure pot or singing kettle—
for Progress brings us (calling us the gainers)
yearly more inescapable containers.

Therefore I've tried to be No One, with an air—
no, not even air—living in Nowhere,
neither tomorrow, now, nor yesterday—
under a sheep's belly, say,
with old Odysseus, crafty knave;
for there's the Cyclops, and this night's his cave.

Suburb Hilltop

Withdrawn from layers of upper air, ice-blue and clear,
the city wrinkles down under its mist
as if in fear,
as if it wished to hide
under those smoky threads which twist
up in the winter afternoon.
They've spun a huge, bruise-colored cocoon
with all the city's larval movements there inside.

I watch a trolley like a worm explore,
halting, over the valley floor,
the lice of traffic and, far away,
black-feelered freighters squatting on the bay . . .
The smoke's cocoon, half curled
back, shows me this new wriggling world,
framed
where my eye has aimed
and pinned it to the valley floor,
visible through my metaphor.

My urban larva, bared to the sharp view
of such iced weapons and the skies,
what will we do
now? Flutter into butterflies?

Canzone for a Tower

The valley buildings there, jammed in a dense
    and unmoved audience,
beady with windows, may observe at will
—now nearly empty for the break at noon—
this full apartment project on the hill,
    where toddlers, out of tune,
scream for their Cinderellas and Jack Horners
just out of sight around the great brick corners
of their childhood—or watch the older ones
    with harmless toy burp-guns,
    fathoming how to feel.
Deaths are imagined; bodies crumpling, real.

Sunlit below the hill, it looks so pretty,
    that tidy dollhouse city,
with no bad smells here and no broken edges;
and there, almost man-sized, straight as a vector
among the lifelike, childlike buildings, wedges
    their omnipotent protector,
the insurance company's tower, said to house and
busy in bright long rooms more than a thousand
employees, calculating every risk—
    a stunted obelisk
    that, rising joint by joint,
like fabled Babel, never achieved its point.

Great base begins, ascends, only to stop.
A gray roof sits on top.
A corrugated pyramid that pinches
inward, like foldings of an old box camera,
it only seems to add a few more inches.
Then, maybe to enamour a
poet who'd say, "Adequately endowed,
it might have poked up through the highest cloud,"
that roof, summoning one last gram of power,
sprouts up a tinier tower,
apparently intended
to show us how the real one would have ended.

How high, had it not been thus telescoped,
might the great tower have groped
out of financial soil, that seemed so fertile?
That shrunk pinnacle gives a sense of distance;
but the whole thing looks drawn in, like a turtle,
out of some scary existence.
Those camera-folds—do they stretch? Stretching taut,
what if, right now, it darted upward and caught
a sputnik? Science tells us there's a chance
a stone building might dance,
fly from its weight, defect
from its form, shriek some dreadful dialect . . .

Song, no; we'll find in grand structures like this
     no metamorphosis.
     They lack an inner pulse,
these high-minded creations of adults.
The stunted angel's rich, but has no wings;
     and under urban soot
     it stays sensibly put;
there's no danger—except from a few, odd,
out-of-the-way, uninsurable things,
     like, say, the Wrath of God.

An Old Performer

Over the big town tonight
three quarters moon travails with dark mist.
The business dist-
rict, to the right,
watches in a chorus,
blinking impassively before us.
Blobs of neon light
fall, filming in tinted drapes,
over the large portly shapes.
There's darkness underneath.
It's like the spiked head of a great dragon
with colored teeth
and fainter glittering scales
sprawling to the left across the horizon,
ready to dine or sup,
belly up.

Mists slide over the chunk of moon, like veils
over an aged, aching dancer, that the bright
glitter on earth, made up of fashion plates,
only tolerates.
Her balance seems uncertain.
Her glow looks hollow-eyed
and pasty, with a touch of applied
orange, and telling shadow.
Below
it's waiting for another show.

Will she go behind her curtain,
while stars are out elsewhere?
Her fading hovers in the air,
the mist.
Only for her those vagaries persist.
Only her glow
detects them, low
where she descends . . .
                                    Lord,
grant us our bawdy dancer! Bored
tonight as we are
with her dull, dumpy charm,

10

she can't do us much harm.
What if she *is* less steadfast than a star?
Like You Yourself—in her profound dishevel,
see: she sinks down to our level
and explores
from obscure, badly lighted stages
our breathing darkness, where the dragon snores
or rages.

Hawks

Wind on the hilltop:
sky rushes up at it,
crowded with hawks as
leaves in the grasses
clinging, loosening,
tumble like sparrows and
newspapers crackle
pinned on the fences,
caught from the sky.

Ah, will the city too
—buildings there—loosen,
tumble like leaves,
all of its lights there
dotting in darkness
swirl up and out like
sparks from a chimney?
Airliners lumber where
hawks are at home,

swiveling over on
wind-gusts balancing—
flick then, off and
way down miles. . . .
O, they dance, they
pirouette like
water spiders
over the footloose
crumbling of air,

walking the wind like
jugglers—jugglers who
stand on their fingers
poised on the looping
puffs they are catching. . . .
Man, were he hawk, how
grimly, importantly
over this wild sky
he would walk!

The Watch

Nightfall on the hill.
Somewhere a siren, wild and shrill,
goes panicking through the streets below.
I search the shadows, hoping for a glow—
something to flash and show
me why I wait here—wait
and think: something's inside me that I hate.

A fire. It's like a sun—
unworldly, yet the heart of one.
A building glows with it, and draws
crowds, men, faces alight, who pass and pause
to watch the scarlet claws
draw earth back into sky,
as through a black tornado's empty eye.

Red-eyed holy birds,
crueler than flesh, subtler than words,
plumed Pharaohs, sun-born worshiped kings,
light, and feed on the solidness of things.
They ride on magic wings.
It is in me they ride.
They're nothing much. They're what I keep inside—

an emptiness I twist
around, attempting to exist. . . .
It's pleasanter kept shut in gloom.
I raise up stones, wall Pharaoh in his tomb,
and try not to exhume
the hollowness it hides—
but the earth shakes, crumbles, and out he rides.

That siren slings its noose
to catch a prisoner on the loose—
me there! I'd have him flashing higher—
darkness is coming—and see the naked fire,
the naked god inspire
his stones, raise up, possess. . . .
Charred walls collapse into his emptiness.

And now the light of day
like a burnt fire sinks away—
and like a melting gauze, has peeled
over the body of the moon, revealed
in a dark starless field,
unterrified and white,
standing out there in nothing but the night.

The Window

Cloud in a dark thick roof spreads overhead,
over suburban valley depths below,
from every closed horizon but the last,
the west; there, let in from the upper sky,
a turquoise emptiness. Here underneath,
roofed in, a landscape caught: headlights in chains
have bound down the dark body of the earth;
low aircraft people space with creeping sparks;
radio tower aerials are blinking.
Of the dim roar only the loudest horns
rise thinly to the hill. Still, lights come on:
how close, how dense, they now seem to become.
All of us here pressed slowly down, congealed . . .
yet there's that band of light across the sky,
the west, windowing turquoise space beyond—
and suddenly I see it's a vast windshield
quietly pushing through the world out there;
and all the little lights are instruments,
flickering on the dark panel of earth,
that no one can decipher. Yet I'm going—
no, not just I, but we, all of us, one—
into that out there, somewhere. Where? O where?

II WAR WIFE

The Conquest

A curious place you found finally to please our senses
after the Continent had witnessed your defenses,

to lead me up that hill where daws and eagles roost
above that town where holy pageants are produced,

as if you'd show me all the kingdoms of the world.
The sun licked over swells of skyline; darkness curled

its long exploring shadows through the waiting hills.
Winds blew, and I lay helpless in the evening's chills.

You were untouched. . . . What could I do there, face-to-face
with countries watching me, and sky, and wordless space

as empty as this solitude in which I live?
Your silence said, "If they are you, what can you give

of them? Those shadow kingdoms in you? Watch them pass!
Can all that space find one white body in the grass?"

Then over a carved table later on that night,
I looked into your face, subdued, saddened, and white,

and was uncomfortable, and became almost cross,
stiff, like a mourner, mourning primly his great loss.

Struggle

It's done; I planned, did it deliberately,
and wormed a place in you with some dull lies.
And now, does a hurt anger in your eyes
whip back? I'll slash the cords you lash to me.

Cast off. Wakes mingled. O sweet piracy—
flesh grappling below rafters, cries. . . . All cries
stop when rising depths choke your replies.
And then blank surface and a white debris.

And so it's over. Nothing . . . then the night.
We sit. I sense you lost somewhere below.
Depths of you move, fingering me with fright,

and the night whirls, goes empty, and I'm wound
down to you, weightless, crushed. . . . O, when I flow
into you, fear comes, both of us are drowned.

In Lieu of Sleep

The bells, bells cleaver out each hour,
quartered and halved
on the chopping block in the tower—
giant stone donation
of our alumnus, the daft
millionaire, to education.
Wine swigs turn me sour,
but I don't sleep.
The bells cut down deep
where I lie, down to the dregs.
O look inside me: coils, curls,
buttocks, breasts, legs. . . .
Put your clothes on, girls.

Go, bells, go greet
her, sleeping down the street;
report those worms that push their dull
white noses through my skull.
They're small. They do no harm.
One's bigger than an arm,
long, pale, undressed,
soft as a breast.
Its teeth are sharp as tears.

I've known her a thousand years.
Somebody stop that tower.
It's raising its arms in the night,
and its clapper ready to bite. . . .
Caught in bed, I cower.

They beat on my head like a book. . . .
O bells
of knowledge!—
stir up the salty wells
in which I cook,
working my way through college—
through volumes, concentrated, terse,
padding me from the universe.
I'll bite, I'll burrow out of here,
scotch wormy fear,
leave her, won't call,
turn tramp, tramp out into nothing at all. . . .

Once more the bells—and there she stands
nowhere, nude up to her eyes' limp stare.
She brings me nothing in her hands.
Darkness is in her hair.

Her smile is pleasant, her face
is white as dough.
I shout at her. My shouts don't show.
Nothing, nothing affects her. . . . No?
Then growing fiercer,
feet in place,
I raise a javelin to pierce her—
draw back my heavy arm, throw. . . .
No trickle from her belly, where it quivers, flows.
She only smiles, smiles,
and won't put on her clothes—
because we've years to go yet, miles
with her inside me still to creep,
miles to go before I sleep.

Sunset

The sun tangles in TV aerials
sticking into soot and sky.
I stop to watch it die
in the street near the hospital's
scrawny trees not yet in bud:
a ghost sun, rinsed in luminous blood.
Once, I remember, it burned that way
before, another August day,
wounding the sky above another
city. . . . We were driving back from the beach,
hoping we loved each
other.

Toys under the sun . . .
down under the sun by the corner, one
walks out from a group of stores, and comes
toward me, and becomes
a real policeman.
And in the sky, above where I'm
standing, a jet pricks, sewing its vapor trail,
its point unseen, its wool fading behind, pale,

like a worm . . . like a man
nosing through time.
Is time blue?   Does the mind
fade out that quickly behind?

At the corner the lights are changing,
and the traffic changes its clumsy dance.
In this, the sun's disk, ranging
from hints of "caution" at its top
to a round, crimson "stop,"
has no effect, although huge and hung high—
only an enormous bloodshot eye
waiting and watching in its trance.
Aerials probe
up into its burning globe.
Ten years we labeled love
with that unwearied eye above. . . .
O hard moment of pending,
what is it we await,
now we have probed into our hate
and wait now only for our ending?

War Wife

Something in me has died that needed you,
and other faces draw before my eyes,
beings who hint at what I'm changing to:
beings that come alive when something dies.

No more the anguish on a barracks floor,
the iron beds, the steel cast into skies;
hollow streets of a Texas town no more;
no more the outer roar and inner cries.

Now these new things flow into, catch my thought.
That face . . . and on the shore a spent fish lies.
Fish swim below—and when may they be caught?
Something must come alive when something dies.

I hear that girl's low voice and know it's true.
Something in me has died that needed you.

Spring Thaw

My once dearest, the snow rots
around stems of last year's forget-me-nots.
Whole years of litter, it seems,
come out when the spring arrives.
Old rooves come back as the snow melts, gleams,
and ice hangs down in rows of dripping knives.
In your smoked room drinking, you melt, gleam,
throw the drink at me, scream.
Twists of rusted iron, clumps
of dead flowers, are born in all the dumps.

There was the snow's first fall,
the strange peace that covered all;
the hurtful things, the spikes, the teeth,
all rounded, mounded, frozen underneath:
the back roads between us choked,
mantled and mute.
We met each other in no real dispute.
Beside the lapsing fire
we'd built and called desire
we sat, said nice things, cautiously joked.
The whiteness like your wedding gown
kept drifting slowly down

out of a gray nowhere to dress
a stubbled barrenness,
but nothing, nothing could be heard.
Flesh had shrunk in from the shell of every word.

I longed for one live bud.
I turn bitter; I find mud
and bare
black moments where
I seem so free—
others where you heap on me
so cumbered, filthy, deep. . . .
The streets hiss. Splashes leap
in the sun, dirty and bright.
I feel hot-fingered light
and March air moving on me, warm and wide.

Slowly you crumble away, trickling inside.

Of Silence

Time and the night wear on here since you've left me
to see if I'll endure your absence badly
and want you back. Now I shall write and tell you.
The silence here engulfs me like a crime
that maybe I committed, but can't quite
remember. Colors here have lost their flavor
diluted in my liquid hours, and words
collapse into the print. I didn't dare
dinner by candlelight, and now my chair
under the lamp shows through its torn worn skin
—its open sores—raw stuffing underneath.
What is it in me now that sickens it?
I think it is infected with the silence.

The phonograph is here, you'll say, to draw me
out of myself. Museum pictures failed
this afternoon, and music etched on records
is like a bank account I dare not spend.
It is as you were: kept with care, reserved,
a nestegg of pretended understanding
that grew at compound interest from the lie
in our first kiss. This comfortable estate
I squander now. Dearest, your melancholy,

like a long lush concerto by some Russian,
repeated much, protested hopelessness—
the kind I never really listened to,
only let play to stop the mouths of silence.

When you were small and left lonely behind
windows in winter, etched and sparred with frost,
maybe you sang, as I did, loudly, frightened,
to scare back nothing, creeping out of corners,
hardly aware of your song's reason, hardly
hearing the sounds you made: so we made sounds
together, each to each, but each unheard
and unaware, since neither knew the reason:
cold fright made us sing. And so we married,
safe from the risk of being too much moved,
and by our quiet fire together crouched,
as in the shadows of a shadowed cave:
and kept at bay things breathing in the dark.

So there was nothing in me that you heard.
I always kept you close, taught you to echo,
kept you by keeping you afraid of me,
pretending it was pretense, loving you.

I taught you many things; you taught me nothing.
When you dared tears for my friend's death, I was
offended; and I dreamed I fell and lay,
rotting in vegetation. There, alone,
you came and wept. Didn't I care for you?
And you—what did you ever do but drag
me down into your flesh, as I'm dragged down,
writing you this to make you pity me
for sending you out, now, into the dark?

Pity me then, since this is what I do!
For in a foreign city once, as night
fell in curved crumbling street, a violin
echoed, taut sinew over singing darkness,
and it wrung down into my soundless flesh.

Of a Young Mother

A woman is playing with her bundled child,
a flower her face, opened and soft and wild.
Why do my eyes find hers in the crowd? This pain
quickened in every springtime with the rain,
the warm rain falling, everywhere the rain
and the seed reaching in its bed of mud. . . .
He seems so small to laugh, who keeps her blood.
Darkly within themselves the smallest twigs are moving.
Nothing is in me for that woman's loving.

I've nothing for her.
I've scratched like a twig at the dead sky,
but what's the good of asking why
and what his miseries will be
when I am here who have denied
in hatred till with withering I died
and buried my longing in the ground
where it first moved in blood and cried,
and now lies deep beyond every sound?

Beyond her singing. . . .
Woman whose singing I denied,
how deep now can I hide
who only knew in terror what I willed
and cannot even guess what I have killed?

Stumps

Moonlight pokes through my skylit ceiling;
    there's wind outside the iced glass, feeling.
I walked today out in the snow-drenched wood,
        not thinking of you,
only how hard and bare the dark trunks stood,
        how tall they grew,

    and found a torn-up stump, bleached as bone,
      lying among brown weeds, alone,
with nothing like it anywhere in sight:
        stub arms that grew,
still twisting palely outward into light,
        and thought of you,

    and how on walks we'd sometimes collect
      dead things like this, lying broken, wrecked,
assuming strange shapes, as a man, a hand,
        some creature of breath,
some fragment, forked limbs, or a hair's strand,
        long after death,

as if they had to keep on growing. . . .
    These trees reach up so high, not knowing
how perilously they reach, nor where they'll arrive,
        till the wind snags them
and tearing up chunks of stone, cracking, alive,
        down to earth drags them.

    It's hard to tell what I tangle still
        here, where the wind howls where it will,
or you back there. . . . Gnarled arms, each without leaf,
        each one too short,
reach out from a bared, torn-up stump of grief,
        sliver, abort.

Branches

Warm night.
Bare branches grasp at the starlight.
Dearest, those stars have no power
to teach
dark winter branches, that reach
out among them, to flower.
And how long have you clutched
despairingly
at what could not be touched
in me?
Those stars so small and dumb.

O—may the dawn soon come.

Beyond the Atlantic

I feed myself well, here beyond the Atlantic—
three buns, wurst, butter,
and ground coffee, for noon breakfast—stutter
to a small circle of inane friends
in two languages, and now and then stay in
on a binge
of lifting life into art,
as rusty arms that hinge
out of a corn husker's mechanically faultless heart
twist husks of hybrid corn up into its bin
for the pigs to eat.
                    Most weekends
my midget auto enters the gigantic
clefts of Black Forest mountains and swerves
under drizzling skies
laboriously up around hairpin
curves,
as a flea up rivery elephant thighs,
to my love, a haggard masseuse,
whom I put to good use,
revealing
my impotence to her unfeeling

womb;
and then I go home.
The Forest gathers and lours
around this town's tinkling towers.

Dearest, I have to keep on wooing
—Rilke says something about it—
amusing
myself with these queer punishments for refusing
to fill your womb with my undoing.
I wouldn't be uncomfortable without it.

I hadn't quite stopped stammering
when we met
in that beerhall where I stalked
through the last war—talked
and tumbled into each other's debt.
You never struck me as pretty;
I kept my qualms.
Now, fifteen years later, there is hammering
here still, building back this phony tourist city
after its one big night of bombs.

Home News

I lie here in this land of krauts,
suffering bouts
of sick pity,
while motorscooters snarl through the city
and, a whole ocean away, you force me
to think. Good, it's time you divorce me.

My stomach's bad.
It's what you had
the month I left.
It stinks, this being bereft—
this morning sickness, giving birth
to at last nothing. O worried earth,
I can't eat these potatoes any more.
Stuffed with pills and elixirs,
I sleep . . . no one will say if I snore
or gnash teeth. Every morning cement mixers
outside grind into the middle of my night
and turn me up, aware
of my smell, to let in air.
I hate the light.

Buildings are sprouting down the street
like plantar warts. Each day in August heat
the ruttish bulldozer has got
itself into another lot,
fusses with walls, tools
in the torn ground; with each swipe
rubble and buried cable drools
out of its mouth, and lengths of broken pipe.
This bombed city is digging up its bones.
Its fifteen years strutting with desperate belief
opened into pits of horror. . . .
                              The groans
have stopped; bombs from beyond an ocean
have given them work. . . . How, after so much grief,
can they still cling with their old monstrous devotion
and build back like that, build and build?
What will they do when their pits are filled
and dark again, dark when it blazes noon?
They'll need another war soon.

My stomach rumbles the new alarms.
My ruined darling,
we grew up in each other's arms,
snarling.
This sickness that I have is yours.
I don't want cures.

Flies

In my dry waterless lair
I can bat flies out of the air
as they spin between the windows, trace
spirals around each other,
and copulate
shining in sunny space.

I've written mother,
told her our only offspring, hate,
the freak,
makes us employers
of suits, courts, and lawyers
with which we flail at the empty air
hoping to strike something there—
man and wife
clenching shut, squeezing their life
out of each other. In thin air it dies.
Last week
my haggard masseuse clamped her thighs
together, and grown tired
of being hypocritically desired,
held them clenched.

I have wrenched
free of so much,
what's left that I dare touch?
Sunlight. Sunlight and flies.
Dark, dark, the murmur of your thighs.
The flies, the flies keep swarming in.
I beat them down in frenzy where they spin.

Elegy

It's time that I deciphered the last traces
of our engagement out in windy spaces
the time my country fought in North Korea.
Marriage was my idea—
because I needed roots
in a prim Texas town
that outlawed prostitutes.
I wanted life more normal,
and so, like war declared, when you came down
I made our marriage formal.
Fanatic nations pursue objects, blind.
I had an image of you, hanging in my mind,
out of your body.

Too gentle, frightened almost, for a nurse,
you could still work. Things might have been much worse.
A homosexual chaplain I'd befriended
married us. You pretended
to like him, and he did the same for you.
Allergic to cats too—
it may have been the kittens in your trunk
more than our cheap champagne that got him drunk.

Who made you more afraid,
he, or the dying man with his face flayed
in your hospital? Keeping those two cute
newborn kittens, you quit without dispute.
There was enough between us—was there not?—
since both of us knew well what pleasure could be got
out of your body.

Kittens consumed our honeymoon. We fed
them with doll bottles; rubbing them, we'd vex
their little bowels to move into Kleenex;
and on each hotel bed
we'd watch their loving romps—
till this all ended in the Georgia swamps.
There, where a captain's crazy English wife
screamed and attacked her children every night,
their eyes opened, they learned to fight for life.
Yours was the female. White
and sickly, she looked cowed.
Maddening how she constantly miaowed.
And yet you wept for her,
when through her tufts of fur
you saw spreading my trowelfuls of dirt,
as if she had been taken, stiffened and inert,
out of your body.

46

The war went on, our whole economy boomed,
and every day I zoomed
over the negroes down
sweating in shanty town
up to the clouds in million-dollar machines—
I, in the elite corps
who'd fight the Next Great War
mostly by automation,
exterminator hired by the Nation
to keep this over-crowding world in check.
While army and marines,
holding it by the neck,
killed Communist Chinese,
I picked our kitten's fleas
and pictured things much better left ignored.
That yellow male survived,
seemingly million-lived
as that unwashed Asian horde
resisting Freedom's probe
from halfway round the globe—
they died with such abandon, backs to their own border.
All I could find was monstrousness, insane disorder,
out of your body.

Then even you grew pregnant—and that cat,
swallowing spiders, wilder—and he spat
back at me, dared to enter
my room at night, tormenting his tormentor—
maybe in quest of rubbing, warmth, or food,
and unaware as loud, unturned-off radios,
booming the news, I needed solitude.
What can one do? One throws
whatever comes to hand, out of one's wits,
and the cat spits.
You feared he might disturb me. Yes, he might.
Sometimes it seemed he cried
as you cried, cried each night
for the tough life inside
you, growing. . . . But one dawn
you woke; the cat was gone.
Who forced him out, then, tempting him, or goading?
Your eyes filled with foreboding—
and General Eisenhower
proclaimed the earnestness of the hour
and said that creeping socialism must be stopped.
We drove to Jacksonville and had the baby chopped
out of your body.

III   APPARITIONS

The Gem

Darkness relents, and dawn
fingers shadowy lawn
and finds a gem of dew
and fills it with sky-blue.

Strange that a thing so small
has room to mirror all:
the house inside the grass,
trees, me, shadows that pass.

How was this thing achieved?
Sun sank; and earth conceived
in shadow, turned from light,
and the drop grew all night

and looks now at the sun—
who sees what the dark's done
and beats down on the lawn
until her gem is gone.

The Stars

Who splattered such a mess against the sky?
Was it the moon who with her spotted eye
watches her shadowed earth as it turns frigidly by?

What force, what anger flung them on the night,
to which they cling now, petrified in flight?
What need they dread but dawn's obliterating light?

They know, they know. Moon-silver, every one,
they're fragments of a world that the moon spun
out of her dead craters to please her mate, the sun.

Sunlight at Work

Sun shines; and stiff snow-islands run
dwindling into cracks and grooves,
steadily down the neighbor's rooves
    to nowhere in the sun;
      and shingles, dark with tars,
trickle with syncopating stars.

Then down from eave and gutter niches,
two stories down, clear now and bare,
they fall, and each drop sews the air
    with sudden, polished stitches:
      out and over they pull;
the fabric is invisible.

Needles of light, flashing so far
downward, threading the huge air
with emptiness—who sees them there
    or knows how bright they are,
      till sunlight makes them glow
with bodies brighter than the snow?

Terra Firma

Broader based than a city block,
more high than an old mansion and more worn,
         this rock
   thrusts out of New England, a gray
      giant, half born
   to sunlight and clear day.
   An icecap smothered it
   for eons where I sit.

Over its bulk of many-stoned
amalgam, which the glacier's brutal kiss
        has honed
   to pink faces, flat, upturned, dumb—
      over all this
   an ant creeps with a crumb.
   Dark scratches back and forth,
   compasslike, still point north.

Some maples lift their leaves nearby,
skeletons decked in spring-green fineries—
            lift high
      their tips of life, now warmed and new,
            to the chill breeze
         and the sky's ancient blue—
         the sky there, so much older
         than even this huge boulder—

      but now how mild we find it grown.
Who can imagine the long glacier's creep?
            Great stone,
      when mountainous dark ice and snow
            fasten you deep
         once more, no one will know
         how hard the slow North's grip
         grinds over your great lip.

Apparition

The pretty girl on the cover
of the magazine on the dump
fades. Leaving her blue eyes
behind, her ochre lips
have bleached, and a ghostly photo,
from the back side of the page,
and broken columns of print
show through her vanished cheeks
and empty hair. Around her
are menacing dark shapes
blotting the starlet's week
(last month). But the clever girl
already has slipped away
and left her hard blue eyes
to stare gemlike, bewildered,
out of the soggy paper,
and mold-islands to grow
—like craters on the moon—
their stringy tentacles,
venturing, as they must,
through glitter, which is dust.

To a Successful Student

When all my other students return safely home
    this June, after their snores and illuminations,
you'll have to remain, I'm afraid, kept here in my mind,
    still running through me, cool and sensitive,
and there I'll meet you through the summer and converse,
    hearing your voice go feeling into corners,
feeling your quiet eyes—the oval of your face
    vanishing under dark and careless hair.

You frightened me, you know. I thought I looked at you
    too much, and after class I feared your touch,
feared others watching while we talked of Greeks and such.
    What if I gave you special things to study?
I was too timid to give more; and now your ghost
    stays in my mind, and in my hand there's dust.

Leaves at Night

Dry leaves are clicking somewhere over darkened pavement
like paws of little dogs running.
The leaves are not on leashes
when autumn comes,
and they will nip the traveler
with memories
of what has withered out of him
and scuttled into doorways
and found out many drains.

Keep them, keep them—you cannot keep them fastened.
No: you must let them run
and smell what crevices they dare;
for all the leaves are pulling from their branches.
Tomorrow a girl may catch one
and bury it in her hair.

Thoughts of a Voyeur

Windows flatly dark. Others glowing
through drawn shades dumbly into the night.
There's one still hollowed out with light,
a carefree light,
looking out over the park
and not abashed to be showing
intimate spaces to the dark,
and there I see a woman pass
gliding behind her window glass.

She stops; and under silent shelf
her hands reach to undo herself.
Her knickknacks watch. The dress slips to a chair.
Her fingers clasp, rove in her hair,
flowing in gold above a lamp,
her eyes darkness, dark her brows.
And she is luminous, stands marble-clear.
I'll tramp
barren for months for this one vision here.

Unhouse
me, since you must,
and draw me to the park's dark dust,
untouched, unreal.
Bright ghost, you give
nothing, only live
as in a mirror's counterfeited space
in which I see a creature face to face
and reach out, touch it—glass is all I'd feel.

And I, shadow like she!
I am her image of me, she, aware
of nothing. . . . Look there!
She swims to me
out of her mirror depth, up to her window,
looks down to me, into this night I'm in . . .
I'm safe. She can't know
I'm here, have been here—or have ever been.

Abroad

The long winter darkness in a strange land.
Stars glitter in the dead grass.
Only the frost.
Only a million mirrors to the moon.

IV SQUIBS

Psychiatric Discharges

I
Why did our hero quit serving his nation?
Insanity: a mutual accusation.

II
O cleansing clinic, modern cloister,
don't wash the sands out of this oyster.
What if they cut him, scratch his whorls?
He makes them cores of all his pearls.

Hymn to an Automatic Washer

O wise God of our fathers,
we love You, yet . . . one question bothers:
   has no one ever quashed
reports that Jesus seldom washed?
   And who can think a greasy
and soiled St. Francis of Assisi
   could cleanly love The Lord?
Shall we imagine he ignored
   those lice between his toes
when he blessed each creature that grows—
   each creature, born or hatched?
Shall we suppose he never scratched—
   though vexed with itching poxes?
Who can resolve such paradoxes?

You can, God of our daughters!—
swirler of heated soapy waters,
    immaculate machine,
where DUZ does everything so clean.
    Cleanse us, if we have sinned,
spin-dry us, lest we flap in wind,
    exposed to harmful germs.
As every snowy shirt affirms
    with underdrawers in chorus,
a new white Idol stands before us,
    rolling its sudsy eye.
America, thy sons reply,
    Down with the old gods! Beat
them into scrap, they're obsolete.

    Warranted washer, prim
in thy enamel and chrome trim,
    we celebrate thy birth.
Whirl on! Protect us from the earth!
    Lead forth this Land's creations
and sterilize the unwashed nations;
    O thou, our helm and shield,
launder those lilies of the field!

To a Poet

SIR, you're immortal, have no fears.
The empty pedantry is real
that haunts your lines, and you'll appeal
to stuffed shirts for a thousand years.

Dactylic Discourse

All who love art will appreciate Virgil.
How does one learn to love art? Read Homer.

Epitaph for a Learned Poetess

One light she never hid:
she knew for all to see
what poems ought to be.
I wish her poems did.

To a Poetess-Judge

Madam, you sit on our city's
lofty poetic committees.
Madam, you weigh in the balance
eager original talents.
Madam, we envy your critical
powers, so nicely political,
yearly to hoist into view
poets as dreary as you.

To One on Friendly Terms with Many Poets

Madam, you're not generous. Were I better
known to the world, you'd find time for my letter.
Unlike a flea, a poet's parasite
needs to be told which carcasses to bite.

In Memory of an Overambitious Poem

That great, meaningless poem! It races
   still through my empty spaces,
   a darkened star, ill starred:
it drew down into itself so hard
it disturbed all motion and all rest
   even to vastest distance—
but in the process it compressed
   itself out of existence.

V CREATURES

Birth in Sussex

Do you hear that hum?
It's spring. It's come.
Life struggles in our chopped bramble hedges.
Life oozes from the young stumps
in cut groves, lifting their fresh white wedges.
Life dreams in the gelded rumps
of bullocks. We've seen the last of the snow.
Over the fields the sunlit tractors curry,
anointing the eager crop.
Lined up like workers in a sweatshop,
Maloney's fruit trees are ready to go.

In barrels and kegs
unfertilized eggs
pour from the all-night dens
of the hilltop's battery hens.
Screaming, its head surprisingly furry,
the baby we didn't abort
appeared last week. Hurry, hurry.
Life may be short.
Out of their holes the animals hop;
Dick walks to town for the family porkchop.

For the warm wind has swooped
on our cottage. Old insect swarms, regrouped
on the cattle tarn, have smelt our infant daughter
and prepare for the slaughter,
and into our gypsy's kitchen poaches
a column of blooded English cockroaches.

A poet like me has to go where
the living is inexpensive,
and that's in the middle of nowhere.
Bearded, celibate, tardy in
friendship and income, I rank great
tomes beside me and read, in the daily *Guardian*,
about the new high bank rate,
congested, pensive,
having achieved autonomy
in England's aborted economy.

But where are the vanished hunters who sung
lost epics in a complex tongue
unknown to Oxford dons
and slaughtered great mastodons?

How can this caved-in hero abide
this dumpy stunted countryside,
plough-churned and sheep-chewed
until the very dirt's turned prude?

He stops in a valley and waters a shrub,
an earwig caught in a dry bathtub.

Willy

Willy, enormous Saskatchewan grizzly—your
   blood partly polar,
tranquil your temper—with only your furred face
   visible in there
propped up over your puddle and pool-rim,
   scanning the crowd for
peanuts: we're all safe on humanity's
   side of your cage-bars.
One of your elbows sits on your concrete
   floor, with its huge paw
coyly supporting your chin, while your eyelids
   droop and your mouth hangs
cavernous, wide as a hillside, opening—
   heavens!—you're yawning.
Seeming so spiritless—so like a man—are you
   mocking us, Willy?

Nuts drop near you, and sometimes your free paw,
	big as a tree-stump,
mossy with hair and with stick-sized claws on it,
	browned and decaying,
darts, and adroitly you sweep one into you,
	Willy—you're much too
civilized, playing obsequious tricks for these
	pestering people:
you who have driven whole ox-herds before you through
	forests and ice fields.
Do you remember your long lone nights on the
	stardark tundra,
now that you're shut in from life and this wearying
	crowd and its clamors?
Bored, Willy? Who can awaken you? ("Up, Willy!"
	someone is calling.)
Peanuts may not be enough. Do you long for some
	tastier tribute?
That, Willy, needs a more godlike behavior and
	("Up, Willy, up, up!")
dignity, Willy; more dignity's needed to . . .
	Willy? What's moving?

81

Nothing is moving; yet all of you—face, paws,
          elbows—is rising.
Mountains of hair there are heaving up under you,
          streaming with waters,
up, up, up out of splashing cascades: dark
          shadowy body
up from the black earth's bubbling depths—and the
          women are shrieking.
How did they dare to confine you, those vermin a-
          live on your shadow?
What is it makes you endure them, O swaying and
          perilous tower,
touching our day with a second of terror, our
          nights with a nasty
Freudian dream? How?—deftly you've caught it—that
          carton of—ice cream!

Makers

Dog footprints in cement,
  the pats half filled with dust,
  stop me to see where they went,
  pressed in the hardened crust—
a big dog plainly, yelping and flying
over that nice smooth new-laid sidewalk drying.

Into the levelled mire,
  what mad pursuit, what races
  after a screeching tire
  have left these fitting traces?
He's no doubt dead now. Was he caught?
Punished? These dogprints tease me out of thought.

Or does he, stiff with age,
  still snooze by winter fires,
  forgetting youthful rage
  and puppy-wild desires
to get the feel of gooey walk—
to plunge in, show off, make the neighbors talk?

Too spirited to mind
his betters, he stayed nimble
and leapt, and left behind
this gay, enduring symbol.
I stand, well tamed, charmed by residual
traces of an untamed individual.

We men must standardize
the things we shape and touch.
Modesty in us shies . . .
we daren't reveal too much.
But be it sidewalk, poem, street,
our souls are always in it, or our feet.

In this dull human plane
an artist's hairy hand!
His shapes, we see, contain
dry pools of dust and sand,
which years will harden and the form
they took preserve—once pulsing, soft, and warm—

a fossil, almost made.
You see in deathless stone
a life long since decayed.
O memoir of a bone,
your maker didn't trot the earth
worrying what his fossils might be worth.

Doctor Cat

He sneaks, absorbed, in coat of black—
our silky scholar on all fours.
In research of a furry track,
there's nothing printed he ignores.

His sensitivity resolves
our lawn's difficult document.
What are his feelings as he delves?
He feels for something succulent.

He goes by rules; no one refutes,
these days, the long established laws
by which so many small disputes
conclude in his incisive jaws.

I've seen what verities reflect
out of his unreflecting eyes;
I've known the kind of intellect
his padded claw may symbolize.

I've heard his argument—his purr
down through the Ages, all gone dark.
Persuasive points—under his fur,
sharpened on furniture or bark—

unearth and bring into the house
a little world he's made his own,
a deft quibble, a squirming mouse.
The life? What's that? Here, sir: the bone.

To a Child with a Top

Pointing to earth, it stands, plump and erect
as you, and with a nervous hum it sings,
seeming to sense what's balanced, what's correct.
The earth's a top: ask God—He pulled the strings.

And when your shrieks of childish revelation
unwind into enlightenment and poise,
you'll find that the earth spins with all creation
on principles you learned from early toys.

That's right; and there's a new depth in its hum.
The globe flickers, and a quick trembling
tells what is missing: *equilibrium.*

Didn't it look so fine, loosed from the string!
Watch now: it wobbles, topples from its pivot.
Its only strength was what your string could give it.

The Swarm

Blowflies explode from nowhere as I walk.
The hot pavement below me glares like chalk.
    Brown on the bleached cement,
I spot the bit of filth from which they flew,
crusted and dry, and poke it with my shoe,
    and it shines wetly. Intent
    buzzings return, bent
    in spirals on the food,
or quick scribbles of shrinking amplitude,

to the fruit, now impossible to find
under its fly-thick, greenly nervous rind.
    I watch them, half afraid.
It's breath-taking. They all crawl and conform.
Such eager industry! The civil swarm
    elegantly displayed.
    Their brightly chained brocade
    of green and golden links
covers a core of rottenness that stinks.

What social sense enables them to meet
on tiny morsels in this desert street
        and settle and belong?
I think they fly on instruments of smell.
Does anything that men do work so well?
        The missile might go wrong
        that fires and feels along
        its calculated flight
to the warm target, swarming in the night.

Yet though men blunder, they can make correction.
O Lord, thy servants labor toward perfection.
        How can they be like us,
these nudging bodies, shiny, tough, and quick?
My flesh shivers, crawls, feeling almost sick.
        Their innards are like pus.
        What if I'm envious?
        Didn't I hope to shine,
pick, glut, in my great country's rapt design?

Even the poet, fishing for renown
and having found it, having played the clown,
     will call his labors blessed,
accept respect, drop his polite defiance,
and praise his country and the works of science—
     and spiral down to rest
     and comfort on his nest.
     O flesh, you're like these flies.
Does no one spiral into empty skies?

One leaves a wife maybe, or quits a job,
flies to a foreign country. . . . Still the blob
     called love and comfort waits—
only to rot when one has lost one's wit
and fortitude and spiraled down to it,
     pulled by the nasty fates.
     Then more and more one hates . . .
     one tires. The sinews twist.
All men grow ugly now. They still exist.

I stamp at them. The flies spiral about
and settle still. No one will stamp them out.
     Give me another sight!
In the next block, clustered on maple trees,
leaves in green swarms are crawling in the breeze. . . .
     At telescopic height
     in far corners of night
     science's watcher sees
fly-spirals mimicked in the galaxies.

Summer House

Is the sun gone? Shadows it made of leaves
no longer sway from darkness under eaves:
the summer's golden coin wears down to winter,
    and skies of worthless lead
     buy up the earth, now dead.
The wind bids, and the roof begins to splinter.

Shut up the shutters, love, and we'll admit
those yellow ecstasies were counterfeit;
but say, when house and heavens go erratic,
    something persists, love, cramps
     through buried cellar damps,
persists when the wind picks into the attic.

From webs that drift in corners of the gloom,
from shadows, walls sweating across the room,
the silence hangs, placid and deep abider,
    and grips. In its caress
     the damps ooze and confess
the rat, the worm, the termite, and the spider.

A maze of useless pipe tangles and squirms
up into rafters like enormous worms.
There must be rain above; these worms are flowing.
        Look: a rat sips. He gnaws
        holding between his paws
a mildewed seed. The air's not right for growing.

So don't be angry, love, that termites bore
tunnels for dinner through our two-by-four.
They're gnawed too: tinier lives in them are swarming.
        In little private nights
        inside them, parasites,
secreting acids, keep them still performing.

While dynasties and summers pass unseen,
they work; they fear the light. But up between
the boards, light comes. When footsteps crossed that rafter,
        all hairs bristled to hear
        perilous sounds so near,
voices alive with long forgotten laughter.

But they passed too. Here all is secure, love,
from change, growing, and dying up above.
A little circumscribed—but useful, clever.
    Come wind, come sun, come rains,
    the cellar still remains,
a part of earth, and earth might last forever.

Jungle War

Weak sun-rays out of winter cloud;
the dusty windowpane crossed once by a dark bird.
In a far room the baby cries aloud;
between us two, no word.

But heightened by the lonely cry,
tropical silence in us sets its traps and harkens.
Old grudges deepen and intensify,
and outside the sky darkens.

Under the books, the knickknack shelves,
the shreds of cobweb that still hold our lives together,
we penetrate the jungles of ourselves.
Bombs burst, touched by a feather.

Can no one stop this dull, mad war?
Each still avoids the other's unimpassioned kiss.
O, we no longer know what we longed for.
Maybe it was this.

Drought

The hushed rush of a bird's wing
over the spider forests of autumn.
    We've had no rain.
Mice amplify, crackling the leaves,
into terrors, which aren't worth finding.
    We try to live,
as the owl circles at sundown,
humming, listening to the leaves.
    We are the hemlocks
by the road, marching into darkness;
we are the dried husks of a summer,
    split open, empty.
Over the red mist in the west
the sky has a thumbnail crack—
    the new moon.

VI   MEMOIR OF A PILOT

Memoir of a Pilot

On May 15, 1956, a Canadian Air Force jet fighter crashed into
a hospital for nuns near Ottawa. The pilot's ghost speaks.

I

Only the winter's coal is still alive
under the rubble, their heaped cellar smoking
still at the end of my jet fighter's long dive
from six miles high, out of control,
let us believe, since not a soul
can know now. Nothing's left: a chimney poking
through vanished floors, a scrap of wall,
a twist of fire escape . . . that's all
of the nuns' hospital here
an hour ago. Crowds gather. O it strains
imagination. Out of nowhere, out of clear
blue silence, thunder flashing the plains,
brick, steel, mortar gone up like oily paper,
and thirty aging sick Nuns of the Cross
a dead loss,
their bones, mingled with mine, a vapor.
Even pure spirit can't disparage
such ruins. Orgiastic hour,
they reach up jaggedly, a broken marriage
to Heaven, scratching at clouds, a topless tower . . .
an end worthy of that machine and I,
seventeen tons of us, plunging through the sky.

Heaven's heavily charged bridegroom has ripped
into the stuffed, be-tissued earth, and sipped
his last communion. Lord of Hosts,
what will you do with all these new-made ghosts,
dropped from the womb where life had held us curled,
the dark caress and murmur of the world?

Finding me hard to bear, earth pushed me out.
I can feel mouths twitching in vague distress
that hurry through me. Were I to shout,
no one would hear. A dog sees me and growls,
jumps into where I am, howls
and runs off. It is my emptiness. . . .
When life went pouring down this gutted drain,
it clung, like crumpled cellophane.

II

Under six miles of layered and streaming wind,
earth filled its fancy costume, harlequined
in acred squares of sunlight, grassed or ploughed,
wired with rails—and roads thread, where cars would glint
too small to see. The cities were fine print
smudged and illegible, as lumps of cloud
erased them, slipping pinkened underneath,
formless as jellyfish, doing no harm
where salmon-silver fighters darted teeth
for their kills. Scrambled on a false alarm,
we'd climbed up high to practice. None must fail
to follow with trained hands his radar's beck

and green bilious glow
and catch the horny speck
of foreign life, creeping through clouds and airs,
as you would catch a flea in a dog's hairs
and crush it bloody with your fingernail.
The dog, my country, cowering below,
whimpers in fright, and heaving its huge brawn,
yelps advertising slogans at the dawn.

I intercepted neatly in a dive
and braced to blackout, pulled back the control.
It didn't move. My last minute alive
began, budging that stick—stuck fast in ground
or ice—and diving faster than my sound
downward, trapped in a beautiful machine,
worth millions, like a weasel in a hole.
Plump girlish clouds came tumbling up to meet me.
I looked into the earth's enlarging scene
—those growing towns—and stopped pulling the stick:
I had a moment left—they all go quick—
one iced moment and tons of fuel to heat me.

III

I never harped on life. It's not a trade
for devotees of living. It's a parade
that pivots round in rank on ordered rank
memory at its hub, a hole, left blank.

I was a presentable young man,
my cheeks pink, my interior unguessed,
blue-eyed, blond, and tan,
fresh from the ice cream parlors of the West,
the vacant girls, the Sunday dreams,
the syrup market loves. . . . Matted blood
on buried altars, beaten back to mud
once more, and naked hunters on the huge
continent watched. . . . Irksome dependencies!
Airplanes furnish an excellent subterfuge
for young men with destructive tendencies.
I dined there, drank, did as my fellow men did,
and in my silvered uniform looked splendid
in sacrificial pleasure. We knew the end,
my friend and I, and then one night my friend,
mixing his drunkenness with steel,
crumpled himself in a mere automobile.

Life gets excited when it senses death.
Wind spins: it is the cyclone's empty center.
Urging through barriers of sound, past breath
of young girls in our ears, we long to enter
the emptiness round which our being swings;
and now the massed
momentum of my shining cleaver-wings,
swinging to earth, has chopped me clean at last.
I drift among my ruins, tuned
to things still coming from the wound.

O but there's nothing. I'd a lust for flight,
to see the spun world tilting from my sight.
I've climbed up into the deep bowl of night
—a heady drink, the dark earth sunk to dregs
below, to sediment, the living mass.
Cities, emerging as I'd pass,
glowed like illuminated easter eggs . . .

. . . the prestidigitater, quick stunter
in clouds, after ten thousand years hunter
once more of monsters below the polar ice,
woolly mammoths from Russia—we, cooler, calmer
than matadors. . . . Once or twice
we thought it might be a bomber.
But no: the magic radar diviner
had locked on an unscheduled airliner.

We were well paid, we chewed on the land's fats,
experts in death, destruction's technocrats.
Over our glassed-in cockpits the wind swirled
with power to tear our eyeballs from their sockets.
Out of our skies, we reached into the world
and found the Godhead jingling in our pockets.
Why should I notice much or much peruse
—since they were something great nations could use—
the boredom in me and the buried rage?

103

Ottawa, crowded with flesh, spread like a page,
rose to me, clearer, clearer; buildings appeared. . . .
I couldn't steer, and yet it seemed I steered
into that great unfolding blossom, a great bee
to suck and sting. I wedged my knee
against the control, and back and forth
we wobbled. . . . We leapt north,
I don't know why—or why, with power
to root up Ottawa's tallest tower,
we had to auger down
into this sordid little town.

IV

The sunny stones of God glint still, still shined,
poor conjured earth. But even in God's mind
a vacancy, a loophole in His System
must gape sooner or later.
I'm not much of a God-hater;
we two died young; I doubt that I much missed Him.
Still, things get made, each with its built-in curse;
and if this manufactured universe,
perched with its rump on nowhere, thinks that I'm
responsible for this crime
—thirty old nuns boomed out of their wits,
the saints among them with the hypocrites—
I'll say: Poke deeper in the piles of time.

Am I the first monk to go off and play
with springs, clocks, the *perpetuum mobile?*
O   upward   striving   urge: cathedral   tower,
stone rocket blasting off on spiritual power,
toting your crazy souls to God's dimension,
I stand before you, God's latest invention.
All in the same cockpit together, we blast
back down to earth. Things grow. We're going fast.

And in the building, one cracked feeble daughter
of God, dreaming the centuries she'd toiled
to reach that barren hour, had asked for water,
whining. Before it reached her lips, it boiled.
And I, puppet avenger, hold unreeking
hands up to say to no one: I'm content.
Forlorn, innocent creatures, torn and seeking
in windy spaces of a continent—
age after age of crying into nowhere. . . .

In the dark building's shade, I see it there:
the dark sprouts light. There is my sun inside it.
Its windows are wounds, spilling strings of fire.
Weakening bricks desperately try to hide it,
leaking into nowhere, higher, higher.
A wall splits into lightenings and bends double.
The deeper flesh peels in bright scrolls, which drift
and bare skeleton floors that lift. . . .

A curl of smoke lifts from this hump of rubble.
Crazed iron steps still dangle, twisted.

Nature abhors my vacuum, will enmesh
me. . . . No. Let me be nothing. I've existed
enough. Soft perplexities of flesh—
if dust must stir to me, if I must own
a shape again, let me be arid stone.